MY POEMS

Poetry or children

By

ELLEN RETOMA

COPYRIGHT © 2021 MY POEMS

By Ellen Retoma

Published by Poetry Planet Book Publishing House

Arranged by Tess Ritumalta

Edited by Marie Ezekiel

ISBN;

978-621-8261-29-7- Hardbound

978-621-8261-28-0 - Softbound

Illustrations used were taken from Pinterest and may contain their own copyrights

DEDICATION

This poetry book is dedicated to all the children who love reading. I want to inspire you to read poems. Most of these poems are based on my personal experience during my childhood days. Others were written with you in my thought, that even we are in such a difficult time as this, I want to rekindle the hope inside you. To continue to dream and hold on to that dream until that day that your aspirations will be a reality.

Happy reading!

The Author

ABOUT THIS BOOK

This Book of Poetry is a compilation of poems for children. This will help them see life from a beautiful perspective, appreciation of nature, and love of the family. To give respect to their parents and value the time spend with them.

This features also a glimpse of Filipino culture and the simple life in the provinces. This helps children grow in perspective of what really matters in life.

This is also useful in teaching reading, literature and as motivation for some competencies in science for the elementary grade learners.

The author is so much optimistic that in this first attempt to share her thoughts with the world, her work would be appreciated.

TABLE OF CONTENTS

CHRISTMAS IN TIME OF PANDEMIC

Christmas: a time so awaited!
Season dream by every child
When lights in various colors
Filled the houses and streets.

It's the time for shopping for families and friends
To visit loved ones
To bring some gifts, hugs, and kisses

But the pandemic changed the course
The usual routines were reset.
Travels are limited
Hugs and kisses are being discouraged.

If Christmas is love
We will not be affected
Try loving someone
Even in absence of tangible gifts

Christmas has its truest sense
When it is in the heart
Love ones in distance are actually not apart from us

It's Christmas in pandemic
That Christmas has the real meaning
Prove your love by offering not wrapped gifts
But knees kneeling down in prayer.

CHILD OF YOUR DREAM

I was born just yesterday
Yet I had already travelled the world
I had seen all the beautiful places
And indulged in bountiful sceneries

I was born just yesterday
But I have met your grandfathers already
I had seen our heroes
And embraced me on their chest

I was just born yesterday
But all the world is in my hands
Including the moon
The galaxies and stars

I was just born yesterday
But I know you from the past
Because I am a child
Born from your dreams.

CHAMPION READER

I am a warrior.
I am victorious.
I fight not with other children
but with evil deeds.

I am a hero.
I am great.
Because I am not afraid to learn
how to read.

I am Superman.
I am Spiderman.
I defend my books,
I take good care of them all.

I am batman.
I am Captain Marvel.
You will be amaze
Because I can read well.

I am a hero
Because I love reading.
I read poems, I read stories
I am a champion
I can read everything!

FLOWERS

Red, pink, and violet
White, lavender, and orange
Oh! surely you rock my heart
to dance in glee.

Flowers in various shape and sizes
Heavenly treasures spread on earth
They are real pictures
Of God's love

Flowers bloom anywhere
Just like God's eyes
that sees us all.
Whom love spreads wide
To all races and kin.

Flowers come in varied colors.
Reflects God's care for all seasons.
Though the skies are gray,
There's a flower to cheer me!

When the rain is heavy,
Flowers just on our way.
Some petals might fall,

Yet, the next day
They will still bloom.

Oh, flowers! How lovely!
Reflects my Creator's love for me.
Flowers! So fragrant!
So as my praise and worship should be.

LEAVES

Green blessings all around
Tiny leaves so nice
Big leaves shade us
Artistic gifts abound
Crafted by the great and mighty hand

Some are long, some are round
Others are elongated and thin
They also come in a cluster
and in singles.

There are leaves that are
Spirally arranged
While in some plants they are alternately fixed.

Green wonders, so refreshing
Relaxing to minds and spirit
Stress and worries flee
Whenever I am with them.

They uniquely sway
As the winds blow
They clap as the rain flow
They whistle with the breeze
Oh, I love the leaves!

TRAVELERS

We travel along with life

In the road of time

We travel along with life

In the bridge of choices

We travel along with life

In the path of decision

We travel along with life

Each day

each hour

each minute

We are travelers!

THE LUXURY I WANT

I wish I could have
the luxury of time in the universe
So that I could write
and write all my thoughts.

I wish I could spend all my days
doing nothing but just writing,
writing and writing.

I want to pour out my brain.
To release the words and letters
That are just sleeping.

There is someone inside me,
Wanting to go out.
A poet untold- that's who am I.

MARSHMALLOWS IN THE SKY

Clouds are like marshmallows in the sky
As the wind blows, clouds move.
Different shapes and sizes
Forming a beautiful picturesque

Clouds make me wonder at their beauty
They are waters actually in gas forms
But why is it they are so beautiful?

They come in various colors, too!
During summertime, they are so white as
snow,
While on a stormy day, they turn into gray!

While during windy days, they are thin
and feather-like
Sometimes, clouds are in layers, too.
But at sunset, they are red and bloody.

BLACK HUNTER

It is so sad to think about my lovely cat
His eyes talk
His mouth speaks
He has a super sweet meow

I love the way he cares for other cats
He keeps sharing
He keeps helping
Oh! I miss my lovely cat
So dark and softy.

His eyes are lovely
His paws are neat
He is so sweet and nice to be with.
I miss you hunter
My cute friend.

THANKS, OH POETRY

When the things to be done seems unending
When all that I have in my eyes are papers,
papers and nothing but papers!
Thanks, Oh Poetry for breaking the monotony.

Thanks, oh poetry for providing a diversion of
thought
That for a while I can relax my senses
To take a breath ...thanks Oh Poetry!

Thanks, oh Poetry for the joy to rise from
within
A product of harmony of texts and letters
Thanks, for the poetry...
I'm at focus once again.

RISING UP AGAIN

No matter how young
are the leaves flowers,
When a catalyst strike
No one could ever hold the stems.

Both the green leaves
and the brown ones
from the trunk are removed.
As the strong wind blows
they will just move and go with the flow.

Though the shedding sometimes causes pain,
discomfort and strains.
Nevertheless, after some sunshine and rains,
A growing life will rise again.

On every lifeless branch,
tiny green leaves grow.
Until a better canopy now is formed
from the old rugged trunk.

ANG IBON

Ako'y masaya
Sa tuwing nakikita
Ibong lumilipad
Gawa ng Diyos na dakila

Siya'y umaawit
Twit! Twit! Twit!
Nagpupuri sa Diyos
Na nasa langit.

LITTLE BIRD

Once I see a little bird

My heart leaps

Oh! flying little bird.

The Lord God had made.

It sings so sweet

Tweet! Tweet! Tweet!

Singing praises to Him

The God of the heavens.

THE SEA

I love the sea
The waters so blue
When summer comes
Where we always go.

The waters so calm
The breeze is so cool.
Oh! I love the sand
And play by the shore!

My sister and I
We run to and pro
Just like the waves
Which come and go.

My mom and dad
Are swimming
While my brothers
Build sandcastle

Oh! I wish every day
Is summer
That by the sea
We always be together.

RAIN

Drop! Drop! Drop!
Rain drops more
My paper-boat
Starting to float.

Drop! Drop! Drop!
Rain drops more
My friends and I
Will go swimming.

Drop! Drop! Drop!
Rain drops more
My clothes are wet
And I want more.

BESTFRIEND

My best friend is my mom
Because she loves me.
She never leaves
Even when gets angry.

My mom is my best friend
She understands me
She forgives my faults
She always hugs me.

When I am wrong
She is sad
She hit me by her rod
But I know it is love.

She corrects me
When I made mistakes
She teaches me
When I don't know.

She cares for me every day
Every night I also pray
Lord, please help my mom
And make her happy.

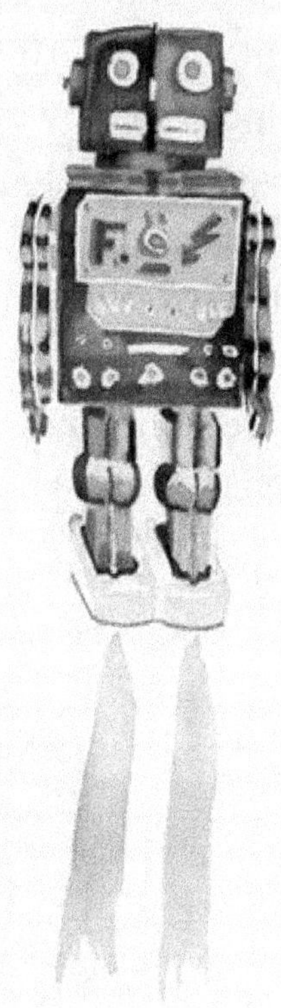

ROBOT

I have a toy
It's a robot
His name is Tony.
It is so cute.

Dad bought it for me.
As a gift for my birthday.
I love my toy
I love my dad, too!

My dad plays with me.
Tony and I
are so happy.
When dad plays here
with me.

DOGS

Bow! Wow! Wow!
Oh, it's Brownie.
Bow! Wow! wow!
Brownie, stop!

Bow! Wow! Wow!
Oh, It's the Puppy!
Bow! wow! Wow!
Puppy, stop!

Bow! Wow! Wow!
Oh, It's Blackie.
Bow! Wow! Wow!
Blackie, stop!

Bow! Wow! Wow!
Oh, my…they're all together
Bow! Wow! Wow!
Brownie, puppy
Blackie, stop!

THE MOON

Mommy, what is that?
Its letter "C"
So bright

Baby, that's the moon
It brightens the night

Mommy, where does it go
During the day?
Does it hide under the tree?

No, baby, it's just there
In the sky.
Staying there above.

We cannot see them
Sometimes they are behind
the clouds
Or maybe at the back
of the land.

It is not always letter "C"
Sometimes it is "O"
Where it lights more
and glow.

COVID-19

Covid-19 go away
I want to be out and play.
I miss my class
Where my classmates and I
Together we stay.

Covid-19 I hate you
You're no longer welcome here
I and my mom wanted to go
To shop and visit the mall.

I miss the smiles of my friends
To see their faces without a mask
To laugh and shout freely
In the playground distance free.

I will go with dad to the park
to eat some snacks
to sip some juice from a straw
without the worry of the cough.

BROWN OUT

The lights turned off
It's so dark all around.
The sounds tuned off
So silent everywhere.

I can't see my mom
I can't see my dad
I can't see my sister
Even my brother.

But their calls me
I hear them say
"Don't move!
Just stay"

But I am so scared
I shouted so loud
My mouth opens so big
When the lights come back.

I am faced at the mirror
I see my mouth so large
My mom and dad laughed
I was ashamed
and I cried.

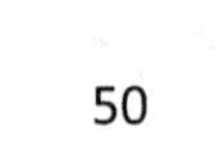

THE CARABAO RIDE

One day, I rode at the carabao's back
It ran so fast that I can't stop
I held on to the rope so tight
When it swam to the mud.

I had fallen from its back
I fell in the thick mud
I sunk into the deep
Where all that I can see
were just clay.

My white shirt turned to grey
My face was so ugly
Where my teeth are just the white
That you can see.

I cried but no one was around
Nobody came to help me out
I just stand and slowly
removed the mud.

I said to myself "Congrats!"
An experience so priceless
Even when I grow old someday
The memory will stay.

WHEN I LOST MY SISTER

It was tragic
It was painful
When I lost my sister.

she alighted from a jeep
one day
when a rushing truck
hit her backpack.

She was dragged
Few meters away
Broken skull
Broken bone, bloody.

She was left on the street
Lifeless and cold.
So helpless
and breathless.

I love her so much
But I just can do nothing
Now, I know she is in heaven.
Happy and pain-free
Dancing with the angels.

www.glory5f

A PRAYER

Lord, I thank you
for giving me eyes to see,
The beauty of the things
around me.

Lord, I thank you
for giving me ears to hear
The sounds of the music
around me.

Lord, I thank you
for giving me a hand
That I could extend it to help
Others who are in need.

Lord, I thank you
For giving me mouth
And a tongue to speak
That I could sing your praise.

Lord, I thank you
For the heart and brain
That I could make
right decisions so well.

Lord, I thank you
For making me this way.
Please just make my life be
For your goodness,
a living testimony.

MY HAPPIEST BIRTHDAY

My happiest birthday was long ago.
There was no cake, no spaghetti
There was no hamburger
Nor a juice or soft drink.

But that was the happiest
You know why?
That's was the day
when my family was complete
and happy.

With my father and mother
both present
All my sisters and brothers
were there.
And when my grandparents
were still alive.

That was the time before
Kidney failure has taken
my father from us.
When at the foot
of the mountain, we lived.

We are carefree,
Simply living happily
Lacking in money
But we're being loved completely.

That was my happiest birthday ever
No presents nor many foods to eat
Just a simple prayer
While happy together
with our ordinary meal.

LOLO BALDING

Lolo Balding is how I call
my grandfather
He is so kind and jolly.

He used to plant crops
Like camote, peanuts and corn.
He lived in a small hut
On the mountaintop.

He was so loving
He always long to see us,
His grandchildren
He is tireless in climbing the hills.

At his old age
He never complains
He is in pain, he still tries to sing.
He never lost his smiles
despite the pains.

Lolo Balding used to tell
A lot of stories and verses for children.
The stories of "Blanca Nieves"
and Ibon Adarna were his favorites.

He told me a lot of stories
Until I fell asleep
Those are the memories
Lolo Balding to me has left.

MISSING YOU, PAPA

There was no single day
That I did not miss you
My father so dear
So caring.

It has been two years
Since sickness stole you from us
Yet, your memories still so fresh
That I could not forget.

My only comfort
Is that I know
While you were here
We showed our love
for you.

Though we miss you
There's no regret
For everything we've done
To make you feel

That you are special
and so dear
just like the way
you did when we're still little.

Now that you're in heaven
From pains and sickness, you're free
With the holy angels
You can sing praises happily.

YOU'RE BORN TO WIN, YOU'RE A WINNER!

You're born to win not to lose,
You're born to gain not for defeat.
You're born is to live not to die,
You're a winner!

You're born to win your problems
To win your trials and pains
To outgrow your weaknesses
and to go out of your shell!

You're a winner-don't you know?
It is not because you're great
Not because you're strong
But because Jesus did it for you!

YOU'RE A TEACHER

You think teachers
are just in schools?
Or just in classrooms alone?
No, no, no, my friend
Absolutely No!

You're a teacher, too!
Friends are teachers.
Mothers are teachers.
Fathers are teachers,
and so are you,

I tell you, my friend, It's so true!
"Why?" probably you'll ask
Because you and me
are made to influence other's lives.

When you share good things
You teach others.
When you care for them
You teach them to live
That's why you're a teacher!

FLY MORE ...

Flap still…a little bit more.
Flap again, flap more!
Keep trying, oh dear little wings
Until you reach the place of your dreams.

Flap more… a little bit more
It's hard, it's difficult I know
But just keep on trying
Oh, dear little wings
Flap to reach the place of your dreams.

It must be tiresome
It might be so hard
But as long as you have
a very good reason
Just fly…fly still
Flap a little bit more.

THE MASKED GEN

We are the masked generation
Of the 21st Century
We live in this era
That we did not choose to be.

We are covered not
because we are afraid,
We wear the mask because
we care.

We are the masked gen
Born in a time of the pandemic
When cruel covid-19
hit our planet,
Just like the past decade.

 We don't know how it came to be
Or who are the culprit to be blamed
All that we know
We are advised to hide.

We are told to secure ourselves
The virus is on the air
Anytime we could breathe,
we follow protocol as directed.

We wear our masks and face shields, too.
Just like when driving, "distancia amigo"
We keep distance and sanitized,
These all we do.

ABOUT THE AUTHOR

Ellen Retoma

(Ma. Elena Dogayo Erandio- Retoma)

A poet from the Philippines archipelago. She is public-school teacher by profession and voluntarily serves as a Sunday school teacher.

Her childhood years mostly spent with nature. She grew up in the mountainous area of Sta. Cruz, Casiguran, Sorsogon, Philippines. Raised by her parents who are both farmers- Gregorio Erandio and Salvacion Dogayo.

Her love for poetry started at her young age. She is fond of reading books, both fiction and non-fiction, including literature and poetry.

Currently, she dedicatedly serves as Teacher and a school leader in a small and remote school in Bulan, Sorsogon, Philippines. She is not just a civil servant but also active in helping people find meaning and purpose of life by teaching them about the Word of God. As a school leader her passion is in innovation and improvement because she believes that every child deserves to be served and treated well.

She is happily married to Richard Retoma. Even though, they were not blessed to have a child of their own, her love for children is great that she enjoyed being with them and always aiming to inspire the young generation achieve their dreams.